Published by Candle Books
an imprint of
**Lion Hudson plc**
Wilkinson House, Jordan Hill Road,
Oxford OX2 8DR, England
www.lionhudson.com/candle

ISBN 978 1 78128 196 3 (UK paperback)
ISBN 978 1 78128 233 5 (US hardback)
e-ISBN 978 1 78128 228 1

First edition 2015

A catalogue record for this book is available
from the British Library

Printed and bound in China,
June 2015, LH06

# The Midnight Visitors

By Juliet David

Illustrated by Jo Parry

CANDLE
BOOKS

It was very cold and dark outside.
Miriam had never seen so many people in the little town.
She was glad she was snug in her cowshed.

When she breathed out, steamy clouds
floated from her damp nose.
Dan the herdsman had long gone home.
Miriam settled herself down for the night.

Tap, tap.
What was that?
Just the wind...
Tap, tap, tap.
There it was again.
Miriam raised her head.
Someone at the door!

"Moo. Moo.
Who's there?"
"Just me and my little family,"
piped a squeaky voice.
It was Rita Rabbit.

"It's freezing, and my Sammy has such a nasty cough," said Rita.
"Any chance we could sleep in your barn tonight?"
Miriam was secretly pleased.
She didn't *really* like being all on her own.
"It's a bit late for visitors," she complained.
"But I suppose you can."

Rita, Ronnie, and their litter of baby rabbits hopped in.
They quickly found a heap of dry hay in a corner.
One by one they dropped off to sleep.

Rat, tat, tat!
Miriam was just dozing off.
The barn felt a bit warmer now and she was *very* tired.
Rat, ta, tat! *Now* what's the matter?
"Moo. Who's there?"

"Ruff Ruff.
It's me – Freddy Fox."
Miriam glanced over at Rita and her family,
all fast asleep in a furry, heaving mound.
"Sorry. It's *far* too late!" she told him.

"Ruff Ruff.
*Please*, Miriam!" barked Freddy.
"All the chickens are locked up for the night.
And it's so cold, I think it might snow."
Miriam went to the door and poked her head out.
"Listen," she whispered. "Rita, Ron, and their family
are asleep inside. There's to be *absolutely*
no hunting in my barn."

"Yes, yes, yes,"
barked Freddy impatiently.
"Just let me in – before my beautiful
brush freezes off."
Miriam pushed the door open a bit wider,
and in slipped Freddy Fox.

Freddy prowled around and around, sniffing the air.
He chose a cosy spot near the cows' feeding box and curled up to sleep.
As good as his word, he pretended he'd not even *seen* the rabbits.
Miriam sighed, then settled down and tried to sleep again.

To whit – to whoo.
An owl hooted.
The wind howled.
The flickering lantern swung.

# Knock, knock!
Miriam jumped.
She'd been dreaming
of a lush, green meadow.

# Knock, knock!
The door shoved open.
Dan's boss, the innkeeper,
shone his lamp around the stable.

"This is it," he said. "It's the best I can do."
*What a cheek*, thought Miriam.
*There's nothing wrong with my cowshed!*
In came a really tired looking man and his wife.
The man went back outside and led in a bedraggled donkey,
laden with bundles and bedding.
"Make yourselves as comfortable as you can,"
said the innkeeper.
Then he left.

*Is this a cowshed or a hotel?*
Miriam thought to herself.
Then she realized that the woman
was expecting a baby – very soon.
She knew the woman
would need lots of sleep.

Miriam moved away from the warm spot where she'd
been lying to make room for the woman.
Perhaps at last they could all get some sleep…

"Whhhaaaa! Whhhaaaaa!"
Miriam woke with a start. Whatever was that?
Then she saw the woman was cradling
a tiny baby in her arms.
He was crying.

The woman fed her little boy.
Then the man wrapped him gently
in a cloth and laid him in the hay
in Miriam's feeding trough.
Miriam felt she was bursting with pride.
Finally everyone settled down again.

Miriam almost dozed off.
Then – way in the distance – she thought she could hear singing.
It was more beautiful than anything she'd ever heard.
So many extraordinary things were happening this cold night!

# Thud, thud, thud.

A lot of running footsteps.
Then, without so much as a knock on the door,
a whole gang of out-of-breath shepherds
burst into the cowshed.

The moment they saw the sleeping mother
and her baby, the shepherds stopped.
Fingers to lips, *shush, shush, shush*.
They stared in wonder.

The mother woke. She checked quickly that her baby was safe.
"Sorry, lady!" said a bold shepherd. "We didn't mean to wake you."
"An angel told us we'd find you here," whispered another.
"He said you'd had a *very special* baby," piped up the third.

By now *everyone* was awake.
Rita Rabbit's family all stared at the baby.
Freddy Fox sat up, stretched, and sniffed the air.
The visitors' donkey nuzzled a wooden post and whinnied.
The shepherds knelt by the baby's makeshift bed.

"Look – we ought to be getting back
 and let you sleep," said one shepherd at last.
"We'll always remember what wc saw here tonight,"
 whispered his friend.

They all tiptoed out.
The rabbits dozed off again.
Freddy Fox pretended
he was asleep too.
Day was coming soon.
But Miriam would never
forget this night.